A PET OWNER'S KEEPING YOUR BEST FRIEND HEALTHY AND HAPPY

Top tips from an expert veterinarian

STEPHEN POSNETT
BVSc MSc(VetGP) MSc MRCVS

Copyright©2013 Stephen Posnett

All rights reserved. No part of this publication may be reproduced, stored in a retrieval system, or transmitted in any form or by any means, electronic, mechanical, photocopying, recording or otherwise without the prior permission of the author(s).

Edited by Tom Stevenson

Cover design and page layout by Mateusz Nowak

Contents

Foreword 5
Introduction 7
   Taking care of your pet's health 9
   Giving your pet a great start in life 11
   Choosing your perfect veterinary surgeon 13
   Looking for the right dog 20
   Preparing your home for your new dog's arrival 25
   Socialising and training your puppy 29
   Introducing your dog to other animals 31
   Housetraining 32
   Basic commands 33
   A few more tips 35
   What to expect at your pet's first veterinary health check 37
   What vaccinations will your pet require? 42
   Parasites 48
   Common health problems 49
   Should your pet be neutered? 52
   Recognising pain in cats 55
   Travelling with your pet 61
   Caring for your pet in environmental emergencies 63
   Dealing with bad behaviour 68
   Don't forget pet insurance! 70
   A great working relationship with your vet 71
Conclusion 74
Appendix: Stressed cats at veterinary visits 75

Foreword

*The **"Pet-Owner-Vet"** bond is special – a fact Stephen Posnett and his dedicated VETCall Veterinary Surgery team take very seriously.*

This strong bond of affection soon grows between you and your new pet. In order to enjoy this relationship for as long as possible, you and your veterinarian play an active role in maintaining your pet's health.

Having said that, it is not always easy for the busy pet owner to find or digest or trust all the pet care information now available from well-meaning friends, acquaintances, the internet and the press. So when the new family companion arrives who should you turn to for trusted, unequivocal pet advice?

Obviously, like your family doctor, accountant or mechanic, you should be seeking out your family veterinary surgeon.

But this is sometimes more easily said than done. From experience I know how busy vets are, having to be not only the general practitioner, but also the consultant, surgeon, dentist, paediatrician and counsellor.

So I congratulate Stephen on producing this excellent home pet guide for his VETCall clients. An exceptional piece of work combining the latest in veterinary science and practice with an easy, understandable and comprehensive guide to help the pet owner in all areas of their pet's health

This book will help you keep track of the most important healthcare measures, including those administered by your veterinary surgeon and those you can carry out yourself.

Over the year it gives a complete picture of your pet's healthcare with advice on vaccinations, routine check-ups and treatments.

A pet owner's guide to keeping your best friend healthy and happy

The information contained is invaluable to you and allows the team at VETCall to provide a super level of care. Please refer to it regularly, share it with friends and bring it with you every time you visit the surgery.

Enjoy!

Alan Robinson

Alan Robinson BVSc MRCVS DMS
Veterinary Business Consultant
Vet Dynamics LLP
www.vetdynamics.co.uk

Introduction

> *"Until one has loved an animal, a part of one's soul remains unawakened."*
>
> **Anatole France (1844-1924)**

Pets are members of the family. I can't imagine a single pet owner who'd argue with this statement.

I consider my role as a veterinary surgeon to be far more of a calling than a career. In many ways, we're an extra emergency service – providing pet owners with a little extra peace of mind about their pets' health and being there to offer support in emergencies.

However, whilst a compassionate, knowledgeable and experienced veterinary surgeon will take great care of your pet, there's plenty you can be doing yourself between visits. It's a great feeling to know you're doing everything you can. Together, you and your veterinarian can provide your pet with the best care for a long, healthy life.

That's why I wrote this book. In the pages that follow, you'll find clear, practical advice about what to look for when it comes to your pet's health, what you can do to keep them healthy and how to develop a great working relationship with your veterinarian. All this information is easy to act on. None of it requires any specialist knowledge or skills and it can be applied to any small animal, including cats, dogs, rabbits, guinea pigs… even chickens!

This information isn't intended as a substitute for regular check-ups with your veterinarian. It's simply aimed at helping you develop a better understanding of your pet's health and thinking about it in terms of their overall wellness rather than just dealing with emergencies, illnesses and injuries when they occur.

We'll be covering a lot of different topics, and by the time you're done you'll be well-equipped to identify your perfect veterinary surgery, develop a great working relationship with them and work together to ensure you and your pet can enjoy many more happy years together…

Stephen Posnett BVSc MSc(VetGP) MSc MRCVS

VETCall Veterinary Surgery, North Chingford, London

Taking care of your pet's health

Here's some good news. Most of the principles behind keeping your pet healthy and happy are universal and apply to any animal. For example, although a cat will need a different sort of vaccine to a dog, the principle is basically the same – taking care of your pet's health in order to deal with problems before they occur.

This is more important than ever nowadays as our pets are living much longer lives. Vaccines have effectively controlled a great number of serious diseases, and improvements in training, technology and medicines over the years means veterinarians are seeing far fewer accidental deaths through road traffic incidents and the like, but more chronic medical conditions.

Microchipping has proven to be an extremely significant advancement in pet care, as stray pets can literally be located in minutes. If you haven't already had your pet microchipped, I would strongly advise you to do so as soon as possible. A microchip is a small electronic device, about the size of a grain of rice, coded with a unique number that is implanted under the skin between the shoulder blades and read by a scanner. Microchips help deter dog and cat theft and allow immediate identification of pets that have strayed or gone missing, so that pets and owners can be reunited quickly. Although it may not be of any immediate benefit, if they ever go missing, you'll be very glad you did!

> **VET tip:** The microchipping of dogs will become compulsory by law in England on 6th of April 2016.

Many pet owners assume the vet is only there to take care of their pet in the event of a serious illness or injury; unless something goes disastrously wrong, they'll potentially go months between visits. The problem with this approach is that it focuses on short-term remedies as opposed to the long-term health of your pet.

> **VET tip:** Register your pet with a vet as early as possible and prevent problems before they occur.

Giving your pet a great start in life

As soon as you bring a new puppy or kitten home, make their first appointment at the veterinary surgery. Regular check-ups will be an important part of your pet's life from its earliest years. This will allow your veterinarian an early opportunity to provide advice on healthcare and treatment. This may not have immediate, obvious health benefits, but it helps prevent serious problems later in life. Don't be tempted to skip this.

> **VET tip:** Be wary if your new veterinarian doesn't offer you practical advice straight away.

Your veterinarian will provide you with advice on a recommended diet, based on your pet's breed, age and environment. Much the same goes for your pet's vaccinations, which we'll discuss in detail later.

This can develop into a full life plan for your pet's healthcare. Whatever is offered at any stage will be highly specific to the stage of life your pet has reached – a Spaniel puppy will have a very different set of health concerns to a geriatric Chihuahua.

The most important thing at this early stage is to allow yourself and your pet to start developing a close relationship with your vet. This is so important for several reasons…

Many pets are scared of being put in a carrier and taken to the vet and if they have friendly, familiar staff to greet them during each visit, they will be much more at ease.

Your pet's health will go through changes throughout its life, so it's beneficial to have someone with an intimate knowledge of their medical history looking after them as they get older.

At all times, you should be sure to act on your vet's advice between visits and make sure your pet is taking any medication prescribed to them, sticking to the recommended diet and following all advice you've received.

Amongst the core skills my veterinary staff possess is that they gain concordance, the shared decision-making process between themselves and the client, and inspire compliance, the client's adherence to recommendations given by veterinary staff to safeguard the health of their pets. Compliance can be improved by simply presenting a client with all available treatment options while offering a clear recommendation, for example.

Choosing your perfect veterinary surgeon

The role of a veterinary surgeon is one of great responsibility, so it's important that you choose one you trust deeply, as they are likely to be looking after your pet's health for many years to come. That's why the decision of which veterinarian is right for your pet isn't one to be taken lightly.

I'd strongly recommend that you investigate as many vets as possible in your area and take the time to visit them personally. Ask plenty of questions and don't be afraid to trust your instincts. If possible, talk to other pet owners in your area, or even the local rescue shelters, and ask them if they would recommend a vet for you – honest feedback from a real pet owner is the single greatest indicator that you will be happy with their services.

Here are some key points to consider before making your decision:

Royal College of Veterinary Surgeons (RCVS)

Veterinary practice in the UK is regulated by RCVS and every practicing veterinary surgeon must be registered with the RCVS. In all professional communications, vets must show the initials MRCVS or FRCVS after their name as this indicates that they are licensed to practice.

But what do all good veterinarians have in common? They don't stop learning after graduating from university—they study further in a subject that reflects their area of interest and which is directly relevant to their work in order to develop their career further, adding to their skills and improving techniques as new discoveries are made in veterinary medicine. Qualifications should be prominently displayed.

A pet owner's guide to keeping your best friend healthy and happy

> **VET tip:** Don't be afraid to ask your veterinarian about qualifications – no good vet will be offended by such a question and will probably be flattered!

RCVS Practice Standards Scheme (PSS)

The voluntary PSS accredits veterinary practices according to the services and/or specialities they offer. Accredited practices undergo rigorous inspection by qualified inspectors every four years. Between inspections, practices may be subject to spot checks.

Surgeries that have achieved PSS have met requirements encompassing premises, diagnostic equipment, laboratory facilities, qualifications and continuing education of staff, dispensing of medicines and health and safety regulations and display the RCVS Accredited Practice logo.

Using an RCVS Accredited Practice means high standards of care for your pet, giving you peace of mind.

> **VET tip:** The VETCall Veterinary Surgery is an RCVS Accredited Practice and also a registered Veterinary Nurse Training and Assessment Practice.

Personal recommendations

Word of mouth recommendations are very valuable as they are usually unbiased and you are more likely to get a true appraisal of the abilities of the veterinarian and the practice in general. Such recommendations could come from a friend, neighbour, work colleague, rescue shelter worker, pet shop owner, dog trainer, groomer, dog walker, boarding kennel or cattery employee or pet sitter.

Most people with pets are approachable if you're new to an area, and are always willing to talk about their pets.

> **VET tip:** Ask around and if the same veterinary surgery comes up repeatedly and is favourably mentioned – that's a good sign.

> **VET tip:** View the websites of your shortlist of potential practices and read their testimonials.

Location

Your veterinary surgery should be as accessible as possible in terms of location. Convenience is important particularly in case of an emergency, if you need to make multiple visits for treatment or to collect medicines. Driving a few extra miles or paying a bit more may be worth it to get the care you want for your pet. Consider good access to public transport.

> **VET tip:** Choose a veterinary surgery that has dedicated parking spaces for clients only. This is a premium feature in London!

Opening and consulting hours

Whichever veterinarian you opt for, make sure they are flexible in their working hours. You can't assume that your pet will only ever get sick between

9 and 5 o'clock on a weekday, so your vet should be available in the evenings, weekends and holidays in case of emergencies without charging an absurd premium for call-outs. Early opening allows clients to drop off pets before taking kids to school or journeying to work.

> **VET tip:** VETCall is open every day of the week and provides a year round, 24-hour emergency service. Emergencies will be seen at VETCall at any time, will always take priority and you will not be directed to another surgery at a different location.

If your pet has to stay overnight, there should be a member of staff monitoring them at all times. Be sure to ask about this.

Meeting the veterinary staff

No good veterinarian should have a problem with a potential client arranging a no-obligation meeting to find out a little more about them, meet the staff and to be shown around the practice. If they say they are too busy or don't seem particularly interested, then it's unlikely your pet will receive a high standard of care from them.

Do staff greet you when you arrive at the surgery?

Pay attention to how nurses and receptionists interact with visitors. Do they smile and greet you as soon as you walk through the front door, or do they seem bored and disinterested? This can reflect on both the standard of care your pet is likely to receive and how easy it will be for you to book appointments or get help during emergencies.

You should be made to feel welcome as soon as you arrive!

What is the vet's attitude when meeting your pet for the first time?

It goes without saying that all veterinarians should be genuine animal lovers who take a keen interest in each and every pet that passes through their surgery doors. They should be naturally at ease around your pet, calling them by their name and enjoying the chance to meet them. They should be in no hurry to finish the appointment and should have plenty of questions about your pet.

They should be highly knowledgeable and be able to answer any questions you have straight away.

> **VET tip:** Prepare a list of questions beforehand.

Equally, your pet should relax quickly around them. Some animals are naturally more cautious when meeting new people, but your prospective veterinarian should display a natural talent for putting them at ease. Remember, they'll probably be looking after your pet for a long time, so seeing someone who they recognise and feel comfortable around will make future visits much less stressful for your pet.

Once again, don't be afraid to trust your instincts (and your pet's!); you need to trust the person who'll be taking care of your pet's health!

Do they specialise in any particular animals?

Check that your veterinarian has the appropriate training and experience with the range of animal species normally treated. Small animal veterinarians deal with the care and treatment of household pets, such as dogs, cats, rabbits, guinea pigs, hamsters, rats, mice, gerbils and hamsters. If you have an unusual or exotic pet you might want to find a vet who has experience with that species.

Will your pet always see the same veterinarian?

Continuity of care is so important when it comes to your pet's health. Being treated by the same veterinarian as much as possible makes appointments less stressful and ensures that the vet treating them has a solid understanding of their medical history.

Certain practices allow their vets to share responsibilities for pets, but in my experience, this should be discouraged.

What is their attitude to alternative medicine?

If you are interested in any form of alternative medicine for your pet, don't be afraid to ask. Your vet should be happy to provide an honest, professional opinion on a treatment's scientific merit in order to help you make an informed decision about whether you want to try it or not.

What sort of state is the surgery?

A veterinarian's surgery should operate to the very highest standards of hygiene at all times and be clean, tidy and odour-free. If you see anything that looks slightly suspect when you arrive, then it's probably time to look elsewhere…

Are they upfront about their pricing?

There shouldn't be any nasty surprises in terms of the invoice you can expect to receive. Although invoices will vary depending on the size of your pet, specialist services and out-of-hours callouts will cost extra, all fees should be clearly established before any contracts are signed.

If pricing is a serious concern for you, certain veterinarians will allow you to pay for extra treatments in instalments to spread the financial burden.

However, this relies on there being a great deal of trust between vet and client, another reason why it's so important to establish a strong working relationship with your vet.

Certain vets also offer 'package deals', which can help ease the financial burden for pet owners.

What range of services is provided?

Are they able to provide advanced services, such as laboratory investigations, MRI scans or complex fracture repair, in-house rather than outsourcing them to other practices? This can make all the difference in an emergency, as these services will be handled by someone who is already familiar with your pet's medical history, potentially saving your pet a lot of stress and you a lot of money.

> **VET tip:** VETCall frequently has veterinary specialists visit the surgery to perform investigations and surgery. This means you won't have to travel to an unfamiliar site to get your pet the care they need.

Are they happy to arrange a referral?

No matter how good your veterinarian is and how much you trust their expertise, there may be times when the input of a specialist may be warranted. If this does arise, your vet should have no problem with referring you to the appropriate specialist.

Looking for the right dog

Dogs are devoted to their owners, providing loyalty and unconditional friendship, bringing a lifetime of fun and happy memories. Owning a dog is not just a privilege; it's also a responsibility. This means more than providing water and food for your dog; it's also about making a lifetime commitment to looking after their wellbeing.

On the other hand, cats are less needy than dogs and as they don't require daily walking, are an ideal pet for busy people, being part of the family for anywhere between 12 and 18 years. Given your protection, care, food and a warm place to sleep, a cat will reward you with his or her very own brand of purring appreciation.

If you decide a dog is right for you, you'll need to choose one – one you stand a good chance of developing a long, happy relationship with. Consider these factors when making your decision:

- **Gender.** If you already have dogs in the house, bear in mind that dogs of the opposite tend to get along better than those of the same sex. However, neutering tends to make this less of a problem.

- **Size.** Consider the size of the dog relative to your home and garden. Large breeds of dog don't necessarily need more exercise but they will always need more space. Consider whether you will be able to stay in control of them when out for a walk – your dog shouldn't be the one walking you!

- **Coat.** Dogs with long hair will require daily grooming, so you'll need to be able to commit to this to avoid the coat becoming matted. Short-haired dogs, on the other hand, require comparatively little grooming. If you suffer from allergies, Poodles are non-shedding and make a good choice of pet.

- **Age.** The younger the dog, the more active it will be, although the trade off is that they will be easier to train. Older dogs will take more effort to train (although it's certainly not impossible), but require less exercise, will be calmer and will tolerate being left alone for longer, making them a good choice for the elderly.

- **Pedigree or mixed breed?** Pedigree dogs fall into one of the seven groups (terrier, hound, toy, utility, gundog, working, and pastoral) as defined by The Kennel Club, each with distinctive qualities that define their personalities, along with specific requirements when it comes to their health and wellbeing. As a result, it's generally quite easy to predict a pedigree dog's personality and health needs as it grows up, whereas this is harder for mixed breed dogs. But mixed breeds are less prone to inherited diseases and tend to live longer (poodles are the longest-living pedigree dogs incidentally, living up to 17 years).

Every pet is vulnerable to disease. However, certain pedigree breeds are known to be prone to particular hereditary diseases that affect their quality of life.

> **VET tip:** DNA tests can identify disease-causing genes that allow breeders to avoid breeding pets that could result in litters affected with disease.

Consider your own lifestyle when choosing your dog. If you are house-proud, don't choose a long-haired breed. Love your garden plants? Avoid terriers. Do you live in a flat? Choose a smaller breed. Ask yourself a few key questions:

- **How active is your lifestyle?** If you lead an active, healthy lifestyle, choose a dog that will relish exercising and playing outside, whatever the weather (a Collie for instance). If not, then a less energetic dog, who is happy to sleep most of the day and only go outside to go to the toilet and sniff the garden, would be a better choice, as energetic dogs can become destructive if left alone indoors for too long.

- **Will your dog come into contact with children or the elderly?** Consider your children's personalities and the needs of any elderly people who live with you or who visit you regularly. Children's personalities vary enormously and a dog who has been brought up with older children may not be used to the rough-and-tumble of toddlers. Dogs that have had a bad experience in the past can be wary of teenagers. If you have loud, boisterous children of any age, you'll need to make sure your dog is comfortable with this. Make a family decision about which age groups of children your dog will be allowed to interact with and ensure you stick to this, for the good of both the children and your dog.

- **What is your financial situation?** Looking after a dog can prove expensive, depending on purchase price, food, toys, collars, leads, bedding, veterinary fees, training classes, kennelling and insurance. For example, the average lifetime cost of a Great Dane is £31,800, while for a Jack Russell, it is about £17,000. Veterinary fees are the main expense with average annual charges of £3,200 for a dog and £150 for a cat. Consider what you can sensibly afford and make sure you can lavish them with plenty of love and attention – that's the most important thing in a pet's life and it's totally free!

As you can hopefully see, choosing a dog isn't a decision to be taken lightly, so do plenty of research before making your decision. Make a list of your preferred characteristics for a dog. Based on this, you can start doing research online and start narrowing your choices down to the breed that best suits your requirements and preferences. There's plenty of free information available online.

Looking for the right dog

> **VET tip:** Attend a dog show to meet examples of breeds you're interested in and get advice from breeders and experienced dog owners.

Once you've identified your ideal breed, it's time to decide whether you want to get your dog from a rescue centre or a breeder. Make contact with breeders or rescue centres in your area and register your interest in giving a dog a home. Don't be discouraged if they don't have an ideal dog for you straight away. Responsible, ethical breeders don't breed often, as their priority is to produce dogs of good health and stable temperament. You may have chosen a breed that is quite difficult to find and puppies from planned breeds are often accounted for well in advance. Be patient – a good dog is worth waiting for!

If you have a good feeling about a particular breeder, arrange to visit their kennels and meet their dogs, as this will give you a strong indication of what your own dog will be like.

> **VET tip:** Breeders should ask you plenty of questions about the kind of home you are able to provide.

Give honest answers. Breeders and rescue centres are very experienced at placing dogs, so the more information you give them, the greater the likelihood of success. Be sure to listen to their advice and take this into account when you make your final decision.

> **VET tip:** Ask plenty of questions of your own when meeting breeders.

Breeders should be experienced at assessing for hereditary diseases common to that particular breed. The information given to you should be incredibly helpful.

Information about the sale or adoption should be handled in writing. The contract should include details regarding fees, neutering, health guarantees, terms of co-ownership, restrictions on breeding etc. It should also include arrangements for what will happen if a placement sadly turns out to be unsuccessful despite your best efforts (this will usually involve returning the dog to the breeder or rescue centre). If adopting a rescue dog, be sure to get all the information available on their history.

Adopting a rescue dog may be an ideal solution if you are looking for an older, less energetic dog. It's a chance to give a good home to a dog who may have been lost, abandoned or mistreated in the past. As a bonus, many rescue dogs will already have been neutered and checked for health or behavioural problems before they are put up for adoption.

Preparing your home for your new dog's arrival

Prepare your home for your new dog's arrival to ensure the transition is as smooth as possible.

A checklist of things to do:

- **Dog-proof your home.** A relatively small amount of effort will give you peace of mind when you need to go out and leave your dogs on their own. Move anything that could be broken or chewed – such as electrical cords, shoes and children's toys – out of reach. Block off areas of the house or garden that you want off-limits.

- **Set boundaries.** A pet needs a secure environment outside especially if you want them to go in and out to toilet. Check garden boundaries (especially the base) and gates for gaps to prevent escape.

- **Remove potential hazards from the garden.** Cover ponds and water barrels to prevent drowning. Remove branches that can splinter and plastic flower pots which shatter when chewed. Ensure there are no sharp edges, nails or hooks sticking out that could cause injury.

- **Remove dangerous plants.** Low spiky plants can cause eye injuries, so either place them out of reach or, better yet, get rid of them. Also, remember that laburnums, lupins, poinsettia, azaleas, rhododendrons, Japanese yew, oleander, ivy, holly, jasmine, foxgloves and clematis are toxic.

- **Remove poisons.** Make sure your home and garden is free from poisonous substances. Dogs and cats often like licking antifreeze as it is sweet and tasty, but swallowing even a tiny amount can quickly lead to kidney failure. Chocolate is poisonous to dogs and is fatal in large quantities so never give chocolate, even as a treat.

- **Create a shelter area.** Dogs need a shelter area for both the summer, when they'll be spending time outside in the heat and warmth, and the winter, when they need to escape the cold and damp.

- **Designate a toilet area in the garden.** Select an area for toileting that is easy to clean up. Grass dies with constant soiling, so consider a sandpit to preserve your lawn. Dog faeces can be disposed of in a black bag with non-recycled domestic waste.

- **Set aside a bed.** Dogs need a secluded, draught-free refuge and territory of their own. Their bed must have soft, warm bedding and be big enough for them to stretch out properly when asleep.

- **Prepare for toilet training.** Place newspaper or puppy-pads at the door where you need your dog to go in and out.

- **Purchase a playpen or cage.** A confined space will keep your dog safe while you're busy with domestic chores and at night time.

- **Prepare your car.** Your dog should travel in a crate, on a seat with a seatbelt or in the very back. Never allow them to stick their heads out of windows when travelling. Never leave them alone in the car on a warm day as they will be at risk of heatstroke.

- **Select a water and food bowl.** Your dog must have water available at all times. Place a water bowl and separate food bowl in a safe place where it won't be accidently kicked.

- **Choose a collar and lead.** Regularly re-check the fit of the collar as your dog gets bigger. As an alternative, consider a harness that fits around the front legs and body with a lead that attaches at the back. Leads can be short or long, although extendable leads allow more freedom of movement.

> **VET tip:** A leather, nylon or rope collar should be tight enough that it will not slide over your dog's ears but loose enough that you can comfortably slide two fingers between the collar and their neck.

- **Provide entertaining toys.** Your dog's toys should be non-toxic, with no detachable parts or sharp edges, large enough to be impossible to swallow. This can prevent a lot of damage to your furniture, shoes or newspaper!

- **Choose a kennel or pet-sitter in advance.** Make arrangements for your dog's care when you're away. Have a friend or reliable pet-sitter tend to them or find a good kennel for boarding. Visit a few different kennels beforehand to check which one will be most suitable. Ask lots of questions, like how many daily walks the dogs get. Once again, word of mouth is the best recommendation, so ask other pet owners in your area where they would recommend.

    When you do go away, you'll need to book a place for your pet well in advance, especially at peak holiday times, as the best kennels are always fully booked.

- **Create a schedule.** Get your family together and decide who will be responsible for food, water, exercise, cleaning up and grooming. Draw up a roster.

- **Pick a name.** Every good dog deserves a good name! Even if your dog already has already been given one by the breeder or rescue centre, older dogs can quickly adjust to a new name if you so wish.

- **Take photographs!** You'll want to take plenty of pictures to document your dog's life, to decorate your desk or screensaver and to send out in postcards. From a practical point of view, a good quality photo can help if your dog ever gets lost.

When your new dog does arrive home, give them plenty of time to adjust. Your dog is bound to feel insecure and frightened by the change in environment, while a puppy may be homesick for their mother or littermates. Show them to their crate or bed, where to find food and water and then leave them alone to explore their new surroundings at their own pace. Don't let every family member play with them at once, as too many pairs of hands touching them at once will scare them.

Socialising and training your puppy

We've already touched on this a little, but it warrants further attention as it's an especially important topic for puppies. Contrary to popular belief, a puppy does not have to have been mistreated early in life to be fearful and aggressive around humans and other dogs later on – a lack of socialisation at the appropriate time is often at the root of this problem. Up until the age of about 16 weeks, all new experiences are exciting for puppies, but after that they will become much more cautious and will have to be treated appropriately if this isn't to manifest as aggressive behaviour.

The domestic dog has evolved through artificial selection from the wolf into the many different types we see today, each of which has different needs. Packs of wolves are led by a male and female pair – the alpha pair – who determine when the pack hunt and rest, controlling the lower ranking submissive members. This so-called 'pack theory' has been extrapolated from captive wolves to domestic dogs, but I believe this is not a fair reflection.

> **VET tip:** Wolves are predators; dogs are scavengers and do not hunt or kill. Use conditioning methods that rely on rewards to build trust rather than instilling fear.

That's why it's important to establish ground rules as soon as your puppy arrives home. Be clear from the outset what is and isn't appropriate behaviour and ensure all family members do the same. Consistency is the key to a well-behaved pet!

Socialising a puppy is all about taking things one step at a time, allowing them to enjoy small, pleasant experiences until they are completely comfortable socialising with others. Make short trips outside each day and let new people offer them favourite treats, so they become comfortable with new people. Offer your neighbours a chance to come and visit, so your puppy can gradually get to know them.

Puppies who become stressed between the 6-16 week socialisation phase may develop behavioural signs (restlessness, panting, trembling), physical signs (defecation, urination, vomiting) and coping behaviours (freezing, hiding, low body posture). Gradually expose them to different people and places (the park, forest, pet shop, school, walks through town) and novel situations (vacuum cleaner, tumble drier, car etc.) on their own terms. The more your dog learns of the world in their early days, the more comfortable they will be, but make sure they don't become overwhelmed.

Introducing your dog to other animals

If you have other pets in the house, don't expect your new dog to get on with them straight away. Introduce them gradually, by smell first and then by sight. Don't try and force them to play together. Give them time to adjust and they will become comfortable with each other.

When they meet with other dogs for the first time, stand nearby so they have a safe haven to retreat to if they do become agitated, and intervene whenever you witness unwanted behaviour. Make sure that the first dogs they meet are friendly, sociable ones who won't leave them feeling frightened and overwhelmed.

As your puppy gets older, all these brief encounters will start having a cumulative effect, so it will grow up to be relaxed and friendly in the company of others.

When it comes to co-ordinating your puppy's socialisation with their programme of vaccinations, consult your veterinarian, as they will be able to lay out a clear timeline for you. Once again, be sure to start the process of socialisation as early as possible.

> **VET tip:** Allow your puppy to mix and socialise with dogs that you know are vaccinated and healthy, such as the dogs of your neighbours, friends and family. This can be done before a puppy has completed their first and second vaccinations.

Your puppy should only be allowed out into the public areas like pavements and parks one week after their second vaccination.

Housetraining

Start housetraining as soon as you bring your dog home for the first time by showing them the designated toilet area in the garden. Introduce a command, such as 'swishhh', which your dog will understand is the cue to use their toilet area when taken outside, repeating it often and offering praise and hugs when they respond correctly. This positive reinforcement will help develop the right habits and routines. Once they have done their business, let them play.

Feed your dog regularly and take them outside to use their toilet area after each meal and whenever they wake up. Your puppy will need to use the toilet area 20 minutes after eating, so don't forget!

Whichever method of housetraining you choose – crate training, paper training or litter box – make sure that all members of the family enforce it consistently. Don't punish your dog for accidents, as this is counterproductive.

Basic commands

As your dog gets older and the fundamentals of good behaviour have been properly ingrained, start training them to respond to specific commands. Training your dog will make your life easier and encourage your dog's desire to learn more. Initially, they will need to learn how to:

- **'Sit' and 'Down'.** This will help you stay in control of them and calm them down when they're waiting, meeting new people or being checked by your veterinarian.
- **'Come'.** This will ensure they come back to you every time when called.
- **Walk on a lead.** No matter how well-behaved you think your dog is, a sudden sight or sound may cause them to run away, putting themselves and others in danger. It's therefore important they get used to walking on a lead as early as possible.
- **Play properly.** Interacting with you should be fun for your dog, but first they need to learn to return to you and bring toys back without any confrontation.
- **Keep quiet.** Don't allow your dog to disturb your neighbours by barking without provocation.
- **Stay on your property.** There should be clear boundaries in place to prevent your dog from wandering off and getting lost.

As always, keep your training style consistent, as dogs get confused if rules constantly change.

> **VET tip:** I recommend that you and your dog join an obedience class as soon as possible, as this can be a great experience for you both. For a puppy, that'll be one week after the second vaccination.

Dog training classes allow your dog to meet others in a controlled environment and enable you to learn correct handling techniques. This will strengthen the bond between you. You may even find that your dog has an affinity for learning and may even be able to compete in obedience and agility competitions!

A few more tips

Bathing

Bathing keeps your dog clean and healthy. Be aware that bathing too regularly can prove harmful, as natural waterproofing oils in their coat will be washed away. If you aren't comfortable bathing your dog yourself, visit a groomer. Only use shampoo if there are problems with an undesirable odour or a genuine medical reason, otherwise just use warm water. If you do need to use shampoo, make sure it is one that has been formulated for pets.

Grooming

This is essential for a healthy coat, although short-haired breeds require much less grooming than long-haired breeds. If your dog's coat needs to be clipped, let a professional groomer handle it.

Trimming nails

This won't just help maintain your floors, it'll help keep your dog comfortable and prevent them from injuring their feet.

> **VET tip:** As a rule of thumb, if you can hear your dog's nails clicking on a hard surface, they will need to be trimmed.

Cleaning teeth

Make this routine and clean your dog's teeth at least every two days. Most dogs have no problem with this if they are introduced to it early. Products like hard biscuits, rope, bones and nylon chew toys are designed to control dental hygiene.

A healthy diet

Don't allow your dog to become overweight, as this will lead to health problems. Allow plenty of opportunity for exercise and a healthy, balanced diet. Don't give in to begging. Ask your veterinarian for advice if you are unsure what to feed your dog.

Attending to changing needs

Your dog's needs will change as they gets older, particularly the diet and level of activity. This needn't be cause for alarm, but make sure you maintain schedule regular appointments with your veterinarian to keep track of your dog's health and get professional advice regarding their changing needs, all to keep your dog happy and content in their old age!

What to expect at your pet's first veterinary health check

Once you've chosen your perfect veterinarian and completed registration, the next step will be an initial health check to assess your pet's health and identify any potential problems. There's absolutely no need to be anxious about this. With dogs, take them for a walk prior to the visit to make sure they are calm and docile and reduce the chances of an accident.

Initially, your veterinarian will ask about your pet's health history, past illnesses or injuries. If you have only just welcomed your pet into your home, make sure you've got this information from the previous owner or rescue shelter. They may also ask questions about your pet's general behaviour and personality. Do they enjoy exercise? Do they find it easy getting up in the morning? These questions may seem mundane, but its all part of the information gathering stage intended to help build a complete picture of your pet's health.

Measuring your pet's bodyweight, temperature, breathing and heart rate is part of the minimum data base. Another vital assessment that is recorded at every pet examination is the perceived level of any pain they may be experiencing.

As part of assessing the nutritional needs of your pet, their body condition score and/or body fat index are measured. There is a strong relationship between excess weight and increased health risks, such as diabetes, cancer, arthritis, heart and lung disease and high blood pressure.

During the head-to-tail, hands-on physical examination, your veterinarian will listen to your pet's chest, feel their abdomen, look in their ears and check the condition of their coat. This will help identify areas warranting possible further attention, such as blood or urine analysis.

The detection of a heart murmur in a puppy or kitten is worrying for any new pet owner. There are several causes of murmurs, all with varying prognoses. Congenital defects and acquired heart disease justify investigation, but some puppies can have innocent murmurs, unrelated to heart disease, which usually disappear by four months. If the murmur persists beyond that stage, investigation is warranted. The advice given to a client will vary according to the cause of the murmur and the strength of the owner-pet bond.

Your pet's teeth will be carefully examined. Four out of five adult dogs in the UK have signs of gum disease. Some 80% dogs over the age of three show periodontitis – inflammation and destruction of the supporting structures of teeth – which leads to tooth wobbling and finally tooth loss. Your veterinarian can advise about a daily dental care programme to improve the health of your dog's teeth and gums.

Your vet will explain the findings. Based on the results of the examination, they'll be able to recommend the vaccinations your pet needs, issues that may need investigating or treating and offer you advice on neutering (if necessary) and keeping your pet healthy and happy between appointments.

Making nutritional recommendations enhances a pet's quality of life and is integral to optimal health. This is especially so if nutrition-based risk factors, such as age, activity level, disease, coat and skin condition and medications received, are found or suspected.

General advice on exercise and information on any illnesses or other health problems that are common to your pet's particular breed throughout their different life stages will help you identify early warning signs.

> **VET tip:** I firmly believe that owner participation can help identify and monitor conditions in a pet. Alterations in behaviour are often best assessed by clients when pets are in their home environment.

Healthy dogs generally have a sleep respiratory rate (SRR) of fewer than 30 breaths per minute and rarely exceed this at any time. Recording SRR, where one breath is defined as one rise and fall of the chest when a dog is asleep (but not dreaming or snoring) can help identify and monitor therapy for heart and lung problems.

> **VET tip:** If your dog's SRR increases from a lower level to >30 breaths per minute, call your veterinary surgeon. This may indicate a heart problem affecting the lungs' ability to get oxygen into the body.

Similarly, although managing diabetes is complicated, you can monitor the blood glucose (BG) levels of your diabetic dog or cat at home using a glucose meter, like those used by human diabetics. BG determination is best done under typical daily conditions, where your pet's feeding, exercise and stress levels are normal.

One common problem with BG testing in the veterinary consulting room is that cats can become severely stressed and refuse to eat when confined to a cage or restrained for a blood test. These are not normal conditions and so the BG values obtained will be higher, so it's important to keep your cat calm in order to ensure an accurate result.

A pet owner's guide to keeping your best friend healthy and happy

> **VET tip:** VETCall can lend you a glucometer for you to measure your diabetic pet's BG level quickly, conveniently and at any time at home. We will train you how to collect a small drop of blood first.

It's important to take your pet back to your veterinarian for regular check-ups and to do your own bit to monitor their health and ensure problems aren't allowed to go unchecked, including studying any educational material your vet provides. Once again, prevention is invariably better than cure and may save your pet a lot of pain and stress.

There are four questions every client should ask their veterinarian at every visit:

1. **What and how much should I feed my pet?**
   Good nutrition has more impact on a pet's health than anything else. As pets go through their different life stages, their demands for nutrients and calories change, so keep up to date.

2. **What vaccinations are needed?**
   I believe in the 3-year vaccine protocol. There is simply no reason now why your dog or cat needs to be vaccinated against everything every year. Vaccines should be based on your pet's needs and lifestyle.

3. **What products should I use to deflea* and deworm* my pet?**
   Not all products are equally effective; some say they're all the same products packaged differently! Ask for the best and safest product for your pet and the environment. Oral products are far more efficient and safer for everybody.

4. **When must I visit again?**
   I'd like your pet to stay alive for a long, long time. Apply that philosophy and have your pet checked every six months.

Join my campaign for better veterinary English! Please don't ask for wormers. We want to get rid of worms, so your pet needs a dewormer!

Finally, frequent visits to the veterinarian just to be spoilt with a treat will help your pet get used to the experience!

What vaccinations will your pet require?

VETCall adheres to the World Small Animal Veterinary Association's vaccination guidelines group (VGG) that strongly recommends that, wherever possible, ALL dogs, cats and rabbits enjoy the benefits of vaccination.

The VGG has defined two categories of vaccination:

- **Core** (recommended) vaccines which pets, regardless of circumstances, should receive as vaccines that protect from severe, life-threatening diseases. Core vaccines for dogs are for canine distemper virus (CDV), adenovirus (CAV-2) and parvovirus (CPV-2). Core vaccines for cats protect from feline panleucopaenia virus (FPLV), calici virus (FCV), rhinotracheitis (FVR) and herpes virus-1 (FHV-1).

- **Non-core** (optional) vaccines are required only by those animals whose lifestyle places them at risk of contracting specific infections.

For example, the UK is rabies free and vaccination against rabies is only given as part of the PET passport travel scheme.

Dogs that visit kennels, grooming salons, hydrotherapy spas and dog shows are potentially at greater risk from 'dog flu/kennel cough' (parainfluenza virus, Bordetella). Leptosporisis (Weil's disease) is a zoonotic disease, transmitted via the urine of rats to humans too. This vaccine is least likely to provide adequate and prolonged protection and must be given annually in the UK, especially for dogs in the east of London, where there is an abundance of urban rats, waterways and dams.

In cats, vaccines for chlamydophila and feline leukaemia virus (FeLV) are administered to cats in multiple-cat environments, such as catteries, grooming parlours and cat shows, especially for cats who have free access to the outdoors.

The estimated UK domestic rabbit population, our third most popular mammalian pet, is around 1.6 million and we don't forget them.

> **VET tip:** A new vaccine for rabbits combines a full year's protection against both myxomatosis and viral haemorrhagic disease in a single inoculation and is given from five weeks of age.

These highly infectious viral diseases are almost always fatal and are spread rapidly through contact with wild animals and biting insects such as fleas and mosquitoes, or the contamination of equipment, bedding or clothing.

Although FCV vaccines have been designed to produce cross-protective immunity against severe clinical disease, there are multiple strains of FCV and it is still possible for infection and mild disease to occur in the vaccinated animal.

There is no vaccine that can protect against virulent FHV infection. FHV can become latent and may be reactivated during periods of severe stress, causing clinical signs in the vaccinated animal or the virus can be shed to susceptible animals and cause disease amongst them.

In puppies and kittens, maternally derived antibodies (MDA) from the mother's placenta and first milk colostrum interferes with the efficacy of vaccines administered in early life. The level of MDA varies significantly among litters. MDA will generally decline by 8-12 weeks of age to a level that allows an active immunological response. Puppies and kittens with poor MDA may be capable of responding to vaccination at an earlier age, while those possessing high MDA levels are incapable of responding to vaccination until after three months of age. No single primary vaccination can cover all possible situations.

> **VET tip:** A recommended basic immunisation schedule for dogs and cats with core vaccines and a minimum of two, preferably three, doses for puppies and kittens:
>
> **First vaccination** at 8-9 weeks of age
>
> **Second vaccination** 3-4 weeks later
>
> **Final dose** at 14-16 weeks or older
>
> **First booster** with core vaccines 12 months later. The 12 month booster will ensure immunity that may not have adequately responded to the initial vaccinations.

This is the optimum model for a committed pet owner who is willing and able to bring their animal to the veterinarian for the full recommended course of vaccination.

Dogs and cats who respond to core vaccines maintain a solid immunity (immunological memory) for many years in the absence of any repeat vaccination. Following this first booster after 12 months, subsequent core revaccinations or boosters are given every three years.

An adult dog or cat who received the basic immunisation schedule but was not regularly vaccinated as an adult will require only a single dose of vaccine to boost immunity. Current vaccine data sheets advise that a pet requires two vaccinations in this circumstance, but this practice is unjustified and contrary to the fundamental principles of immunological memory. On the other hand, this approach is justified when an adult dog or cat's vaccination history is unknown and where serological testing of such an animal is not performed.

These considerations above do not generally apply to the optional vaccines and particularly not to vaccines containing bacterial antigens. Leptospira,

What vaccinations will your pet require?

bordetella, chlamydophila products and parainfluenza components require yearly boosters for reliable protection.

An adult dog or cat may today still be revaccinated annually, but the components of these vaccinations may differ each year. Typically, core vaccines are administered triennially, with chosen non-core products being given annually.

> **VET tip:** Vaccines should not be given needlessly. Instead of offering triennial core revaccinations or boosters, VETCall offers the alternative of triennial serological conversion (antibody) titer testing as a simple, reliable and cost-effective assay for dogs (CDV,CAV,CPV) and cats (FPLV,FCV,FHV).

In practice, blood test sampling can be part of an annual health examination in place of boosters and is preferential to unnecessary vaccination and its potential for adverse reactions. It provides clients with the assurance that their pet is protected and that the duration of immunity (DOI) can be many years – possibly for the lifetime of the pet.

Seronegative animals should be revaccinated and retested. If they again test negative, they should be considered a non-responder and possibly incapable of developing protective immunity.

The protection afforded by the FCV and FHV-1 vaccines does not provide the same efficacy of immunity as the FPLV vaccines – feline core vaccines should not be expected to give the same robust protection, nor DOI, as canine core vaccines

Most subcutaneous injections, including vaccinations, are given between cats' shoulders and this is a reported site for the formation of feline injection site sarcomas (FISS). The infiltrative nature of these tumours means that radical, extensive surgical resection is often necessary to attempt removal, which often comes with a poor prognosis.

> **VET tip:** VETCall has a practice policy that cat vaccinations are administered through and under the skin, and not into the muscle, of the left abdominal wall during one calendar year, then alternated with the right side the following year. The skin of the lateral abdomen represents the best choice, as FISS that might arise at this site is more readily excised.

An adverse event is defined as any unfavourable side effect or unintended consequence associated with the administration of a vaccine product. This can include injury, toxicity, lack of protection or a hypersensitivity reaction. Whether or not the event can be directly attributed to the vaccine, it is reported to the Veterinary Medicines Directorate by us.

Vaccination of individual pets with core vaccines is important, not only for protection, but also to reduce the number of susceptible animals in the region and the prevalence of disease, based on the concept of 'herd immunity'. Efforts should therefore be made to vaccinate a higher percentage of cats and dogs.

By encouraging the yearly vaccination of pets, veterinarians are able to recognise and treat disease earlier than might otherwise have been the case. In addition, the annual visit provides an opportunity to inform clients about new and important aspects of pet healthcare.

We're shifting both the emphasis and client expectations from just an annual jab to an annual health examination! We stress the importance of all aspects of a comprehensive, individualised healthcare programme. Emphasis is placed on a detailed vaccination review, a comprehensive physical examination by the veterinarian and individualised pet care. The importance of dental care, proper nutrition, appropriate diagnostic testing, behavioural concerns and parasite control are all addressed.

For aging pets, senior care programmes are increasingly popular. There is no evidence that older dogs and cats that have been fully vaccinated as puppies or kittens require any extra specialised programme of core vaccination. Immunity can be boosted by administration of a single vaccine dose. By contrast, aged animals may not be as efficient at mounting primary immune responses to novel vaccine antigens that they have not previously encountered. Studies of UK dogs and cats vaccinated for the first time against rabies for pet travel did show that more aged animals failed to achieve the legally required antibody titre.

Early detection, particularly of neoplasia, and management of breed-associated disease can significantly improve the quality of the animal's entire life. Pets with chronic medical conditions require periodic examinations and testing. Pets receiving medications require monitoring of their therapeutic blood levels and organ systems. A system of recheck protocols for chronic diseases and medications can be included in an annual health examination and reminder systems can be used to improve client compliance and, accordingly, pet care.

Parasites

Aside from discomfort, external parasites (fleas, ticks, lice, mites, mange) and internal parasites (roundworm, hookworm, whipworm, heartworm, tapeworm and lungworm) cause serious diseases. There is a wide range of anti-parasite products available and it is critical that one or more products are selected, with your veterinarian's advice, to manage parasites your pet is likely to encounter.

VET tip: An easy-to-give, flavoured, chewable tablet with rapid onset and month long persistence, even after swimming or washing with shampoo, is currently the treatment of choice for treating fleas in dogs and cats. The tablet kills fleas quickly enough to stop them from laying eggs in the house.

Lungworm is an emerging fatal disease, with clinical signs related to the respiratory tract (coughing, exercise intolerance, shortage of breath) and bleeding problems (bruising, prolonged bleeding from wounds and nose).

Lungworm is spreading beyond traditional regional 'hotspots', with 50% of diagnosed cases occurring in young dogs. Contributory factors include:

- Urbanisation of foxes, a natural reservoir of lungworm

- Movement of host dogs in and out of hotspots

- Rainfall and damp conditions providing an ideal breeding ground for slugs, frogs and snails – the intermediate hosts. Dogs are naturally inquisitive and keen to pick them up.

Although laboratory detection methods are rapidly improving, it's far better to play safe and select the right anti-parasite product early on.

Common health problems

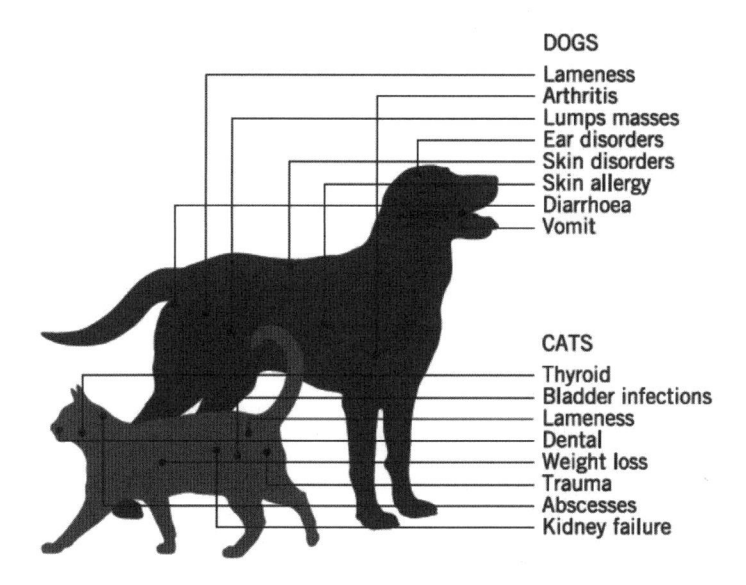

```
DOGS
— Lameness
— Arthritis
— Lumps masses
— Ear disorders
— Skin disorders
— Skin allergy
— Diarrhoea
— Vomit

CATS
— Thyroid
— Bladder infections
— Lameness
— Dental
— Weight loss
— Trauma
— Abscesses
— Kidney failure
```

Common health problems in order of frequency in dogs and cats (PetPlan 2012)

Arthritis is a painful, non-curable, progressive disease of joints leading to loss of joint cartilage that makes most normal movements such as walking, running or even just lying down much more difficult and painful. It is estimated that 20% of dogs older than one year have arthritis. A multimodal approach to lifelong therapy aims at improving quality of life by providing pain relief, reducing inflammation, maintaining joint mobility and preventing further progression.

Skin problems are common amongst pets and the most common reason for pet owners seeking veterinary help – unsurprising, as the skin is the largest organ of a pet's body. The first signs of a skin condition, no matter how trivial, may be an early warning sign that heralds something more serious – a flea bite, an immune-mediated condition or a tumour. The only way you'll know for sure is to have a veterinarian investigate.

Allergies are often frustrating to diagnose and treat and can be caused by external parasites, infection, adverse food reactions and atopy. A detailed medical history is therefore an important part of a dermatological case and questions should cover age, breed, indoor/outdoor environment, seasonality, travel history, contact animals, diet, previous treatments and response, weight loss, diarrhoea etc (most vets are excellent listeners at times like this).

Ears are part of the skin and otitis (inflammation of the ear canal) is common. Management includes medical and surgical options.

> **VET tip:** In my experience, inserting ear wicks soaked with medicines into a flushed ear canal is an extremely useful alternative to daily topical treatment for pets who cannot tolerate this due to the pain.

In middle-aged and older cats, a raised thyroid level is the most common endocrine disease. Careful planning is required for treatment, especially for cats with kidney failure, as they commonly occur together and have complex interacting effects. It is initially prudent to treat this medically, or by an iodine-restricted diet, as a gradual resolution is better tolerated than an immediate one.

Kidney disease affects 30% of cats above ten years of age. Unfortunately, a diagnosis is often only made when at least 75% of kidney function is lost. Symptoms (poor appetite, increased thirst, weight loss, dehydration) are non-specific.

Common health problems

> **VET tip:** Weigh cats ten years or older every three months. Weight loss of more than 5% is a significant indicator of ill health.

> **VET tip:** Simple urine tests measuring specific gravity and protein levels provide an early diagnosis of kidney disease.

Cats need the freedom of the outdoors to exercise, hunt (a need so fundamental to them that it usually persists very strongly, even in the most well-fed of pets), find stimulation for their highly advanced mammalian brains, explore, socialise or defend their territory against other cats, but unfortunately this makes them vulnerable to injuries like cat bite abscesses and leg wounds.

Take the time to familiarise yourself with your pet's patterns of eating, drinking, sleeping and toileting. Any major variations in these patterns could indicate illness and should be reported to your veterinarian. You should be aware of common health problems in your breed, how to prevent them and how to recognise their onset. For example, some giant breeds of dog are prone to stomach bloat, while some short-faced breeds are susceptible to breathing problems. Your veterinarian will be able to provide you with information about which signs or symptoms you should watch for.

Should your pet be neutered?

When your pet does reach the age when you can consider neutering, discuss this in detail with your veterinarian, as there is an awful lot of superstition and rumour floating around on this subject. Neutering is an integral part of general healthcare for young pets and is the most common surgical procedure performed by veterinary surgeons in first-opinion practice in the UK.

Neutering is about far more than preventing your pets from having unwanted litters – there are many behavioural benefits as well, such as helping ensure a calm temperament and preventing scent marking, inappropriate urine elimination, hypersexuality, roaming and aggressive behaviour from developing later. It can also make dogs considerably easier to train.

In both cats and dogs, there is no scientific evidence to suggest that having a litter will change a female's character in any way, so there is no need to put off neutering for this reason. Furthermore, there are health benefits to neutering for both males and females.

For example, males have a reduced risk of developing testicular cancer, enlarged prostate gland, perineal hernias and anal tumours after neutering. Testicular cancer is the second most common tumour type in dogs, especially in dogs with retained testicles.

A reversible alternative to surgical castration for dogs, which also provides a way of testing the effect of castration on testosterone-related issues, is a slow-release implant, as easy as microchipping, that causes temporary infertility for six or twelve months. Clients who find surgical castration undesirable for emotional, social or cultural reasons should consider this 'chemical castration'.

> **VET tip:** A chemical implant is a reversible alternative to surgical castration for dogs.

Females will not be at risk of uterus infections, mammary tumours and 'false pregnancy'. In the case of cats, both sexes will have a lower incidence of lower urinary tract disease and be at a significantly lower risk of contracting FIV (feline AIDS) and FELV (viral leukaemia) from contact with infected cats.

Puberty in cats is typically between 5-8 months of age, yet queens as young as four months can become pregnant. The timing for neutering is therefore extremely important.

> **VET tip:** Neuter cats at four months instead of the traditional six months; it is associated with lower complication rates, shorter surgical time, lower surgical morbidity and quicker recovery. This should ideally take place two weeks after completion of the second vaccination to allow full immunity to develop before being exposed to potential disease.

> **VET tip:** Spay bitches from four months of age and before their first season or oestrus.

This 'early neutering' is recommended for maximum benefit and longevity. If a bitch does have a season, she can be spayed three months after the end of her first season but before her second season. The incidence of mammary tumours increases with each season and is the second most common tumour in bitches after skin tumours.

The risk factor most commonly recognised as a cause of obesity is neutering because of decreased metabolism and activity, due to lower oestrogen levels in both males and females coupled with increased food intake. Early weight control is important (cats start to gain weight and body fat within two weeks of neutering) and it is easier to prevent weight gain than to lose fat.

> **VET tip:** Advanced diet foods, clinically proven to safely and naturally improve metabolism in dogs and cats, are currently the preferred way to control weight.

Male rabbits can be castrated when their testicles have descended, from about three months. Females can be safely spayed from four months of age so long as they're in good health and weigh at least 1kg.

Recognising pain in cats

With widespread improvements in healthcare and nutrition, cats are living longer, healthier lives. However, this trend has created a real need for effective and safe treatments for chronic, progressively painful conditions, such as osteoarthritis, which causes reduced movement and activity.

It is often difficult for veterinarians to recognise and assess pain in cats. As the masters of disguise, cats are excellent at hiding signs of illness or pain and tend to avoid attracting attention until the problem becomes so serious that it is unavoidable – a misguided survival instinct. In the absence of obvious symptoms, diagnosis requires veterinary examination – a challenge even for experienced clinicians, as cats are generally less cooperative than dogs (as many cat owners will readily attest!).

It's therefore vital that you choose a veterinarian who is used to the cats' unique personalities and knows how to make an accurate diagnosis. Observe how your veterinary surgeon examines your cat, as a practice with cat-friendly staff and facilities will understand their needs and display obvious empathy with you.

When treating your cat, your veterinarian should:

- Spend time on the consultation and examination (15 minutes at the very least).

- Show interest in your pet and have a calm, confident, soothing approach.

- Stroke and talk to your cat before lifting them from their cage or basket; cats are usually most content when they dictate the timing of interaction with humans! Allowing your cat to come to them is a very good way of ensuring they view your vet as a friend and cooperate during the examination.

- Have a veterinary nurse who is equally confident with cats provide assistance if needed. A thick towel should be at hand to cover your cat's head if they need to be calmed down.

- Avoid actually restraining your cat unless absolutely necessary.

- Perform the examination in the position the cat is comfortable in, whether that's standing, lying in a carrier with the lid removed, or being held by you.

- Be willing to ask you to leave while the examination is being performed, as some cats are calmer if the owner is not present.

This should take place in a secure consulting room that is quiet, away from noisy dogs, ventilated to remove alarm scents left by previous pets, free of 'hiding places' where your cat could get stuck, and on a table surface that is soft and not slippery.

> **VET tip:** VETCall staff observe behavioural changes and postural signs to assess a cat's level of pain, both of which are an integral part of pre-op assessment and post-op care. Fear and stress worsen pain, so blankets and toys from home, blankets and boxes to hide in and synthetic facial pheromones are employed to help keep your cat comfortable.

There are three categories of pain:

- **Acute pain** occurs suddenly in response to injury, trauma, a tooth abscess, orthopaedic or soft tissue surgery and disappears once the painful stimulus is removed and the injury is allowed to heal. Painkillers are administered to relieve this sort of pain

- **Chronic pain** is characterised by persistent pain, even when there is no longer any lesion that could cause this. This was originally intended as a time-based definition (a pain that lasts for a long time) but must be thought of as a pathological disease, which is where an accurate diagnosis is needed, as therapy cannot rely solely on painkillers.
- **Persistent pain** is caused by a persistent lesion linked to the consistency of the pain stimulus and can wax and wane. Pain relief can help.

Osteoarthritis or degenerative joint disease is an example of persistent pain that has only recently been recognised as widespread in cats. A diagnosis of arthritis is sometimes supported by painful joints, when examination may or may not actually reveal radiographic signs of joint damage, due to the apparent mismatch between clinical examination and radiographic findings.

> **VET tip:** Not all forms of osteoarthritis are painful in cats.

Instruments used to help identify painful joints in cats include force plate analysis, pressure-sensitive walkways (which measure the amount of force generated by one movement), accelerometers and collar-mounted activity monitors.

> **VET tip:** I firmly believe that owner participation improves the chances of a successful diagnosis of joint disease pain. Alterations in voluntary movement and behaviour are best assessed by clients when cats are in their home environment.

Fortunately, most cat owners are keen to learn how to recognise pain in their cats and will readily act on their veterinarian's recommendations if they are involved in the decision-making process regarding treatment.

For this reason, I begin my diagnosis by having the owner list their cat's regular physical activity before they began exhibiting signs of pain. Cats are creatures of habit and features like jumping, general movement, playing, running, climbing up and down the stairs, walking, sharpening their claws, grooming, using the litter tray and hunting will generally display a high level of consistency.

Owners then mark activities on their list that have been altered or reduced. For example, a cat with painful elbows may be able to jump up onto the sofa, but reluctant to jump back down again, or to walk down the stairs, and will typically resist all attempts at encouragement.

Postural changes of a cat in pain might include adopting a hunched, tucked-up posture, a low head position, angled and half-shut 'squinty' eyes and drooping ears, or lying out flat and unresponsive, uninterested in their surroundings.

Other indications of pain might include:

- Grumpiness when being handled
- Withdrawal
- Stiffness
- Weakness
- Dull, matted, scruffy coat
- Excessively long, thick or brittle claws,
- Changes in behaviour (such as aggression in a previously placid cat)

- Less tolerance of people
- Sleeping more, especially in one place
- Muscle wasting
- Failure to move to the litter tray to toilet

The same features are used again to monitor activity after pain medication has been introduced. A 'trial-treat' approach, using an approved painkiller, is always a good option in my experience. The cat is assessed at the start of treatment, then re-examined around two weeks later to allow the treatment to take effect and for the owner to reassess their condition. In this way, a system of monitoring activity and mobility, pre- and post-treatment, is developed and tailored to the needs of the cat. Typically, this will result in an improvement if the right medication is chosen.

> **VET tip:** I favour the creation of individualised pain treatment plans for pets as I don't believe there is any such thing as a 'one-size-fits-all' solution.

For cats, such plans might incorporate:

- Assistance with grooming
- Keeping claws neatly trimmed
- Monitoring bodyweight to prevent from becoming overweight
- Introducing low-sided litter trays, much easier for arthritic cats to use
- Physiotherapy
- Nutritional supplements for healthy joints and tendons
- Ramps or small steps to make getting round the house easier

It's important that you and your vet maintain close contact in order to prevent your cat from suffering any unnecessary pain and ensure any problems are dealt with quickly and appropriately.

Travelling with your pet

> **VET tip:** I often say that "Proper Prior Planning and Preparation for PET Passports Prevents Poor Performance" and nowhere is this truer than when travelling with your pet to ensure your holiday plans are not derailed because you couldn't get a pet passport in time! The VETCall Veterinary Surgery has three government-appointed official veterinarians to provide pet travel advice and issue travel passports. We administer a rabies vaccination that only requires a booster every three years.

The laws have recently changed to make travel with your pet easier, cheaper and quicker, as the UK aligns its scheme with the EU-wide pet movement system.

Animals travelling within the EU <u>still have to be</u>:

- Microchipped before being vaccinated against rabies

- Vaccinated against rabies

- Issued with a pet passport three weeks after the rabies vaccination to enable travel to and from EU countries

Only dogs have to be treated against tapeworms not less than 24 hours and not more than 120 hours (1-5 days) before their scheduled arrival time in the UK and the treatment recorded in the pet passport.

A pet owner's guide to keeping your best friend healthy and happy

But no longer need:

- A blood test after the rabies vaccination
- Treatment for ticks

Areas like the Mediterranean coast, where there are sandflies and ticks, carry the risk of your dog being bitten and catching serious infections, such as leishmaniasis, unless your vet provides appropriate protection.

If your pet is travelling in a carrier, make sure they've had a chance to get used to it well in advance, so it isn't a new and scary experience.

Caring for your pet in environmental emergencies

It's impossible to predict what the future holds, but there are still a number of things we can do to be better prepared for disasters such as fire, snowstorms or flooding. Pets are not allowed inside Red Cross centres or civilian emergency shelters for health and safety reasons, so you'll have to have alternative measures in place in case you and your family are forced to evacuate your home – if it has become unsafe for you, it will almost certainly be unsafe for your pet.

Here are some practical things you can do to ensure your pet will be well looked after in the event of an emergency:

'Animals Inside' sticker

An 'ANIMALS INSIDE' sticker simply alerts anyone who arrives at your home in an emergency, be it neighbours or the emergency services, as to what animals are present in the house. This way, there is no confusion regarding whether or not any animals need to be rescued, something that can make all the difference in a life or death situation.

> **VET tip:** Put an 'ANIMALS INSIDE' sticker at your front door.

One important point: if you do manage to evacuate your pet during an emergency, be sure to write 'EVACUATED' on the sticker as you leave, so no-one puts themselves in any unnecessary risk by entering the house to try and rescue them.

Identify your pet

It could be that you'll find yourself separated from your pet during an emergency, so it's important that you make them easy to identify. At the very minimum, they should have a properly fitting collar with an identification tab that lists any medical needs.

> **VET tip:** A DNA profile of your pet, from the simple swipe of a cheek swab, is the ultimate in individual identification and could be essential for identifying your pet if they are lost or stolen, then subsequently recovered.

Once again, I would strongly recommend that you have your pet microchipped as it's by far the most accurate way of identifying them, and will maximise the chances of the two of you being reunited.

Put them on a lead

Any sort of emergency can be very frightening for pets, causing them to behave unpredictably. This is the last thing you want when you're trying to deal with an already stressful situation, so make sure you have a lead at hand.

Familiarise your pet with their carrier

In the case of smaller pets, like cats and rabbits, it may be easiest to put them in their carrier when evacuating your home, whether that's a specially made pet carrier or an appropriately sized sports bag. Make sure they are already used to being in their carrier and won't become agitated.

Emergency supplies

You can't guarantee what supplies will be available in an emergency, so prepare a set of emergency supplies and make sure the whole family knows where they are kept. This would typically include:

- One week's worth of food
- Litter tray plus litter (an old roasting dish can be used as a substitute if necessary). This is absolutely essential for cats.
- Toys and chews to keep pets (especially dogs!) happy
- A warm blanket
- Bedding
- Cage liner
- Carrier (one for each pet if possible)
- Disposable bags for waste
- Food and water bowls, plus liquid soap and disinfectant to clean them
- Bottled water, in case fresh, clean water isn't available
- Two week supply of any medicine needed, including proper instructions

- Copy of your pet's veterinary records to help ensure continuity of care should they need treatment at a different practice. Keep these in a waterproof container.
- First aid kit
- Recent photograph of your pet for identification purposes and to make 'lost' posters should they go missing

A temporary caregiver

Choose a trusted friend, neighbour or relative who already gets on well with your pet and give them a set of spare keys and a list of emergency instructions. They should ideally be at home when you are away to ensure there's always a friend nearby to take care of your pet in the event of an emergency, or should you be taken ill or hospitalised. Why not trade responsibilities with another pet owner?

A safe place

Make sure there's a safe place arranged for your pet in advance in case you are unable to be there for them in an emergency. If there are friends, relatives or neighbours who would be happy to take care of them, that would be ideal. Alternatively, your vet may be able to provide you with a list of trusted catteries, kennels or rescue centres that you may be able to come to an arrangement with. Check which hostels and hotels in your area allow pets.

Your will

Make sure your will contains provisions for the care of your pet in the unfortunate event of your death. Don't assume that a friend or family member will automatically step in to take care of them.

A final checklist

- Bring your pet indoors at the first sign of an emergency – it's far too easy for them to become disorientated, wander off and become lost.

- Plan an evacuation route and telephone your safe place in advance of departure.

- If your area is prone to natural disasters, such as floods, plan accordingly and identify which are the safe rooms in your house.

- Ensure there's a supply of fresh water. If necessary, fill up the bath, so uncontaminated water is always available.

Dealing with bad behaviour

As much as we love our pets, sometimes they do just behave badly for no apparent reason. Fortunately, this can usually be handled with minimal fuss, especially with the support of your veterinary surgeon.

Look for patterns that will help you identify what's triggering the unwanted behaviour. For example, if your dog starts barking and tugging at their leash when out for a walk, what could it be that sets them off? Children? Food? Once you have got to the root of the problem, you and your vet can start taking appropriate measures to change their behaviour through training.

A good way of correcting unwanted behaviour is through something called 'remote connection', where they start to associate the unwanted habit with something unpleasant. For example, if your pet regularly chews on the furniture, you could try rubbing those surfaces with aloe gel, or a similar unpleasant tasting substance, until the habit is broken.

This is far more effective than physical or verbal punishment, which you should never resort to. All this is doing is making your pet afraid of you, so they'll continue with the unwanted behaviour when you aren't around and will soon be uninterested in returning your affection.

Bad behaviour indoors may turn out to be a case of simple boredom, cured by providing your pet with new toys and entertainment, or longer walks in the case of dogs.

It's as important to reward good behaviour as it is to deal with bad behaviour. For example, if you have been working hard to train your puppy not to bark when the doorbell rings, offer it a treat and plenty of praise and attention the next time it rings and remains on best behaviour. It will encourage them to adopt the same behaviour in the future and, as an added bonus, will help bring the two of you closer together.

Beyond this, there are very few hard and fast rules, as the right solution will depend so much on your pet's age, breed and personality. Putting a sensitive, easily frightened cat in the garage as a punishment would not be advisable for instance, as it would likely stress them out and lead to further behavioural problems in the future.

If your veterinarian has been allowed to get to know you and your pet well, they will be well equipped to advise you about the right way forward and will support you in order to make sure your pet's behaviour doesn't become a challenge. Make sure your vet is aware of problems as early as possible, as the earlier you deal with behavioural problems the better. The longer you leave it, the more ingrained the bad habit will become and the harder it will be to change.

Don't forget pet insurance!

I'd strongly advise you to get pet insurance in place as early as possible. The cost of veterinary treatment for ill and injured pets can mount up quickly, especially as the science is becoming more sophisticated.

> **VET tip:** The client care manager at VETCall will guide clients when it comes to arranging insurance to ensure you pay for exactly what is needed. Even better, she will even make claims on your behalf, saving you a lot of time and effort. If you are a bonded client, we will arrange for the insurance company to pay us directly and you only settle the excess.

Consider taking out a life-long policy, as you can continue to claim for treatment of ongoing illnesses or injuries regardless of how long they persist. Some policies only cover a year at a time, which can become expensive if your pet will need continuous treatment.

There are many different policies available offering insurance for all manner of species, illnesses, injuries and problems (although vaccinations, neutering, dental problems, pregnancy, congenital and pre-existing conditions are not usually covered). Pet insurance can also cover things such as recovery costs if they are stolen or lost (including a reward for their safe return) or boarding costs, should you yourself be unable to take care of them.

> **VET tip:** A new pet can be a fun and rewarding experience, but if your pet suffers an illness or injury, it can also be expensive. VETCall can arrange four weeks' free pet insurance to help cover the cost of unexpected veterinary treatment.

A great working relationship with your vet

Your pet is likely to see the same veterinarian for a number of years – possibly even for the duration of their entire life. That's why it's so important that you, your vet and the rest of the practice staff develop a strong working relationship. This shouldn't be a problem if you've put a lot of thought and effort into choosing a vet, but here are a few tips to help you develop rapport with your veterinary team.

Show up on time for your appointment

It's terribly frustrating for vets when clients miss appointments without explanation. Not only does it mean they are missing a chance to examine your pet again, but that appointment could have been given to someone else, possibly for something more serious.

Make sure you put your appointment in your diary as soon as it is booked. Vets love punctuality! Many practices send text or e-mail reminders for this reason.

Always be polite

It's terribly stressful when your pet is ill or injured, but no matter how upset you are, never take out your frustrations on your vet and their staff. It only makes their job harder.

Bring your pet to the vet in a carrier

Even if your pet is quite happy and relaxed at the vet, other pets in the reception may not be as well behaved, so bring your pet in a carrier to avoid any trouble.

Don't disturb your veterinarian out of hours for problems that can wait

Although any good vet will have their own emergency service and be willing to treat pets out of hours if a problem is serious, don't use this as justification for calling out of hours for minor problems that can wait. Similarly, don't expect an instant diagnosis over the telephone – it's impossible for any vet to offer a definitive diagnosis unless they've had a chance to examine your pet.

Always call ahead

Even in an emergency, make sure you call the practice to let them know you're coming. Don't show up unannounced, as your vet could be in the middle of an appointment with someone else or in the operating theatre. Calling in advance will allow the practice to make immediate arrangements.

Contact your vet at the first sign of trouble

Don't ignore any early warning signs. If you're concerned about your pet's health for any reason, schedule a veterinary appointment. There's nothing worse than watching a pet die of an illness that needn't have proven fatal if it had been treated earlier.

Refer your friends

Many veterinarians rely heavily on word-of-mouth to gain new clients, so show your appreciation for all their hard work by telling your fellow animal lovers about them.

Focus on one thing at a time

Veterinarians need to be highly focused to make a diagnosis, so resist the temptation to jump from topic to topic during your appointment and focus on the main thing you have come to discuss. For example, if you have booked an appointment to discuss a sudden loss of appetite, wait until your vet has made the diagnosis before you ask them about the vaccinations they'll need for your family holiday.

> **VET tip:** Make a list of things you'd like to discuss during your appointment and label the ones that are a priority.

Make sure the right person is present at the appointment

The family member who brings your pet to the appointment should be the one best able to explain the problem and most familiar with your pet's medical history. In fact, I'd advise you to try and have the same family member bring your pet to every appointment, as this will minimise any chances of miscommunication and ensure your vet is better equipped to make an accurate diagnosis.

Bring in one pet at a time

If you have multiple pets then schedule separate appointments for them, as this will help your vet focus intently on one of them at a time and not be tempted to rush things.

Conclusion

I hope this book has provided you with plenty of helpful information about looking after your pets and ensuring they live a long and happy life.

I would like to believe that a long-lasting partnership between you and your veterinary team will develop, benefiting the wellbeing of your pet, if you follow the advice contained in the preceding pages.

In closing, let me return to the most important point of this entire book – that your pet's health needs to be a long-term consideration. Do not focus solely on treating serious emergencies, as by doing this you run the risk of allowing health problems to develop to the point they are untreatable without even realising it. Health screening will improve a pet's quality of life, detect disease at an early age and hopefully prolong their life.

Your veterinarian is going to have an important role in your pet's life. There are going to be regular visits from puppy- or kitten-hood, to junior, prime, mature, senior and geriatric old age. Fortunately, if you choose the right veterinary surgeon and make sure your pet receives regular check-ups, there shouldn't be problems. Refer back to this book whenever necessary and be sure to take a proactive approach to keeping your best friend healthy and happy.

I wish you the very best and hope I'll get a chance to meet you and your pets in the very near future!

Appendix:
Stressed cats at veterinary visits

Ominous hissing, mournful meows, defensive scratching and biting, upset bowels – many cats get stressed when it's time for a veterinary visit. Travel and arrival at the veterinary surgery has been identified as a key area of friction for cat owners, but here are some tips to help your cat relax and enjoy the visit...

The cat carrier

Never travel with a cat loose in the car. Choose a robust carrier, either plastic covered metal wire or hard-plastic carrier, and not so large that your cat falls about in it.

Removable tops make getting cats in and out of the carrier easier. Simply undo the side latches or securing pin, lift off the top, wrap your cat in a thick towel (preferably one that smells familiar), set them inside and replace the top. This eliminates the need to force your cat inside.

Make the carrier smell familiar and reassuring by trying the following tips:

- Leave the carrier with the door removed out in your house so your cat can access it any time.

- Make the carrier inviting by putting a favourite blanket, toy or some clothing that smells of the cat's favourite person.
- Every now and then, lay a few treats inside the carrier.
- Spray the basket and contents with a synthetic feline pheromone, which helps cats to feel secure, at least half an hour before you go
- Wipe a soft cloth around your cat's face to pick up their scent and wipe this in the corners of the carrier.

The journey

- Cover the carrier with a cloth during the journey.
- Secure the carrier in the passenger footwell or on the passenger seat using the seat belt.
- Drive carefully so that your cat is not thrown about.
- Refrain from listening to loud music.
- Stay calm – talk quietly and reassuringly. Cats are clever at picking up tension from their owners!
- Don't let them eat before the visit and take some spare bedding in case they are sick or soil their carrier on the way.
- Avoid bumping the carrier.

Take you cat on a few stress-free trial runs around the block, gradually increasing the amount of time spent in the car. Reward your cat with a treat for being a good passenger. Arrange a free-of-charge 'happy visit' with your vet to give your cat the chance to get used to the sounds and smells of the surgery and meet the staff.

In the reception

- Keep the carrier covered.

- Choose the quietest possible location. Place the carrier high up, not on the floor (cats prefer to be up high). Avoid dogs.

- Don't put your cat face to face with another cat, as this can be stressful for them.

Going home

- As much care needs to be taken of your cat on the way home, so all the same tips apply.

- Strange smells from the surgery on a cat can make other cats anxious and aggressive, but wiping your cat with its own scent can help mask hospital smells.

Every pet is unique.

So is their owner.

Their world, lifestyle and success stories are unique.

This is why we like to get to know them, listen to them and create a strategy and budget to meet their individual, specific needs and those of their pet, now and in the future.

We call this the 'VETCall Experience'.

So keep talking to us. We'll keep listening.

Located in North Chingford, London, VETCall Veterinary Surgery is an independent, first-opinion general small animal veterinary surgery, open every day of the week, providing a year round, 24-hour emergency service. Health and wellness is an ongoing process in order to ensure that you and your pet can enjoy the most special gift – the gift of tomorrow.

We therefore believe in establishing long-term relationships with our clients and their pets rather than just treating emergencies.

As founder Stephen Posnett said:

"A client once said to me: 'I don't care what you know until I know you care' and I think that principle is vital in creating good relations with our clients."

Our veterinary surgeon 'animalogists' have over 65 years of collective experience between them and are still constantly looking for new ways to broaden their skills and offer your pet a super standard of care. Not only that, we are an approved member of the Royal College of Veterinary Surgeons Practice Standards Scheme Accredited Practice and a registered Veterinary Nurse Training and Assessment Practice.

To find out more about us and to arrange your appointment, visit our website:

www.vetcall.uk.com

VETCall
Veterinary Surgery

www.vetcall.uk.com